# The Most Beautiful Roof in the World

# The Most Beautiful Roof in the World

## EXPLORING THE RAINFOREST CANOPY

### Kathryn Lasky

PHOTOGRAPHS BY *Christopher G. Knight*

GULLIVER GREEN / HARCOURT BRACE & COMPANY

*San Diego   New York   London*

Grateful acknowledgment is made to Jack Schultz for the photograph
of leafcutter ants; to Raphael Gaillarde/Liaison International for the
photograph of an inflatable raft and dirigible; and to H. Bruce Rinker
for the photograph of Meg Lowman aboard an inflatable raft.
All images are used by permission.

Library of Congress Cataloging-in-Publication Data
Lasky, Kathryn.
The most beautiful roof in the world: exploring the rainforest
canopy/Kathryn Lasky: photographs by Christopher G. Knight.
p.  cm.
"Gulliver Green."
Summary:  Describes the work of Meg Lowman in the rainforest
canopy, an area unexplored until the last ten years and home to
previously unknown species of plants and animals.
ISBN 0-15-200893-4
ISBN 0-15-200897-7 (pb)
1. Rain forest ecology—Research—Juvenile literature.  2. Forest
canopy ecology—Research—Juvenile literature.  3. Lowman,
Margaret—Juvenile literature.  4. Plant ecologists—United
States—Biography—Juvenile literature.  [1. Lowman, Margaret.
2. Rain forest ecology.  3. Rain forests.  4. Ecology.  5. Ecologists.]
I. Knight, Christopher G., ill.  II. Title.
QH541.5.R27L375   1997
574.5'2642—dc20   95-48193

G   F   E   D
F   E   D   C   B   (pb)

*Printed in Singapore*

*Gulliver Green® books focus on various aspects of ecology and the
environment, and a portion of the proceeds from the sale of these
books is donated to protect, preserve, and restore native forests.*

The display type was set in Leonardo Hand.
The text type was set in Fairfield Medium.
Color separations by Bright Arts, Ltd., Singapore
Printed and bound by Tien Wah Press, Singapore
This book was printed on totally chlorine-free Nymolla Matte Art paper.
Production supervision by Stanley Redfern and Pascha Gerlinger
Designed by Christopher G. Knight and Camilla Filancia

*We would like to thank the following people for their participation and invaluable help in making this book: Dr. Meg Lowman, director of research at Selby Gardens in Sarasota, Florida, and her two sons, Edward and James; Jeffrey Corwin, the field natural-ist at Blue Creek in Belize; and Edward Lowman Sr., who helped to build the skywalk at Blue Creek.*

*In particular, the author of this book would like to express her heartfelt thanks to all of the people mentioned above, who helped her make the ascent into the canopy despite her fear of heights.*

*— K. L. and C. G. K.*

Pioneer in
the Rainforest

MEG LOWMAN climbs trees. She has climbed trees since she was a little girl in search of insects, leaves, and flowers, and now it is her job. Meg is a rainforest scientist, and her specialty is the very top of the rainforest, the canopy.

During the past ten years Meg has spent at least five days a month in the treetops, which adds up to six hundred days. And this does not include the approximately ten days every month she spends at the base of trees looking up. Meg wants to know about the relationships between plants and insects in the canopy. She is especially interested in herbivory, leaf and plant eating by insects and other animals. She wants to know which insects eat which leaves and how their feeding affects the overall growth of the rainforest. To answer these questions she must spend a great deal of time either up a tree or back in her laboratory, studying samples. Meg's lab is at the Marie Selby Botanical Gardens, a rainforest research center in Sarasota, Florida, where she is director of research and conservation.

PARTS OF A FLOWER

Meg cannot remember a single day in her life when she wasn't either looking at or studying a plant, leaf, flower, or insect—except possibly those days when she went to the hospital to give birth to her two sons, Edward and James. Since Meg was six, she has been fascinated by the natural world. As a child she had a bird's nest collection, a rock collection, a shell collection, an insect and butterfly collection, and a bud collection. Her bedroom was stuffed with outdoor treasures. Her great love was flowers; in the fifth grade she was the only child in her class to enter the state science fair. She made a wildflower collection and won second prize.

When Meg was ten years old, she was intrigued by two women: Rachel Carson, one of the first environmentalists, who studied and wrote about the delicate relationships in the web of life, and Harriet Tubman, the most famous "conductor" of the Underground Railroad. Threading through the countryside and deep woods on long, frightening nights, Harriet Tubman guided countless African Americans out of slavery to freedom. Meg read that she often navigated by feeling for the moss that grew on the north sides of trees. But it was not only moss that she had to look for. She had to know which berries and nuts could be eaten, which could make the difference between starvation and survival. She had to know how to find a swamp to plunge into when slave-hunting dogs bore down; the sulfurous mud and slime could disguise a human scent and confuse the dogs. She had to be attuned to the environment in order to guide her people on their perilous journey. Harriet Tubman, says Meg, was a pioneer field naturalist, one of the first women field naturalists in this country.

WHEN MEG is at Selby Gardens, she busily sorts, classifies, and prepares the samples of plants, flowers, and insects she has brought back from her explorations in rainforest canopies all over the world. She has a special permit that allows her to collect many rare specimens, some of which are brought back live and continue to grow in the Selby greenhouses. Selby has one of the largest collections of orchids and bromeliads in the world.

SOMETIMES Meg brings back parts of plants—leaves or blossoms. These she must carefully preserve by pickling or pressing. To pickle plant parts she puts them in a solution of alcohol and water. Although their color might change, the flowers retain their three-dimensional form for study.

To press a plant specimen she folds the flowers and leaves carefully in newspaper, then places them between sheets of cardboard, where they begin to dry out. Back at Selby the drying is finished in low-temperature ovens. Finally Meg glues them down on special acid-free paper. Each preserved plant is carefully tagged and labeled and then put in the herbarium, a plant library.

To gather species of plants and insects, Meg has climbed ropes to pluck leaves, sailed aloft in hot-air balloons to gather orchids, swung on trapezes through the foliage, and even hung over the side of an inflatable raft resting on the canopy. Meg has tried most methods of ascent in her exploration of the canopy. And it has been exciting; she has not only found marvelous insects but has joined the butterflies, swung with the spider monkeys, and peered into the magical little frog ponds at the tops of trees in the tanks of bromeliads.

For a human being, ascending to the canopy is not easy.
There is so much to conquer: gravity, stinging ants, rotten trunks,
and thorns. For years rainforest scientists stood in the deep shadows on the forest floor, looking up as occasional shafts of pale
green light broke through. They could only wonder about the
canopy, brilliantly lit, noisy with bird life and the chatterings of
monkeys. They knew that the canopy was the "powerhouse" of the
rainforest, the place where most photosynthesis occurs and where
95 percent of the biomass, the living things of the rainforest, is
produced. The canopy is where rainforest life begins. Yet for years
it remained out of reach. Even deep-sea exploration was easier.

The rainforest canopy has been likened to an undiscovered continent, a kind of last frontier. Since the mid-1980s better technology has been developed, offering new ways for scientists to overcome the natural obstacles of gravity, ants, and thorns. Such scientists, however, must be strong, fearless, and physically fit as well as smart and hard-working. They must be as skillful as any mountaineer, perhaps more so, for the cliffs they ascend are made not of rocks but of leaves and branches of enormous elasticity. These women and men are the pioneers of a newly discovered continent as they feel their way up to the brightly lit canopy.

Out of the Shadow
and into the Light

Deep in Belize, in Central America, there is a place called Blue Creek. Almost every month nearly 40 inches (102 centimeters) of rain falls. Blue Creek is considered one of the most humid places on the entire planet. In this shadowed world, pierced occasionally by slivers of sunlight, are more varieties of living things than perhaps any other place on earth. Within a 16-foot (five-meter) square there can be upward of two hundred different species of plants.

And there are animals, too. Bats swoop through the canopy. Vipers coil among buttress roots, waiting in ambush. A rare and mysterious tree salamander slinks into the petals of an orchid. Poison dart frog tadpoles swim high above the forest floor in the tanks of bromeliads.

The rainforest is a timeless, uncharted world, where mysteries abound and new or rare species appear like undiscovered islands. Within the tangled vines under the rotting bark of fallen trees, caught in the slime and mold of decaying vegetation and fungi, life teems with ceaseless energy. When a tree falls, the stump rots, bark loosens, and new creatures move in and take over the altered habitats. It is the very diversity of the rainforest that allows life to thrive everywhere, to spring back with a rush of opportunistic species to fill the gaps.

Meg Lowman believes that science is the machinery that runs the earth. She explains, "I think that science is really the way things work, and that's exciting. It is important to understand the bigger picture of our planet and where we live, how it functions, what we do with it, and how that will have impact."

When Meg wants to have a close look at the machinery, she goes to the rainforest, and recently she has been coming to Blue Creek. Meg worries about the machinery. Although it seems invincible, although she can track a new swarm of ants rushing into a tree notch to fill a gap that was not there the previous day, she wonders how strong the machine really is. How many species can be removed before it will break?

Viewed from an airplane, the top of the rainforest at Blue Creek looks like a field of gigantic broccoli. The bright green florets are actually the emergent growth of the very tallest trees. The crowns of these trees extend above the canopy in the layer known as the pavilion. The pavilion is to the canopy as a roof is to a ceiling. From the emergent growth to the floor of the rainforest is a drop of 150 feet (46 meters) or more. Meg wants to go to the canopy, a layer below the emergent one. At Blue Creek a canopy walkway designed by specialists in rainforest platform construction has been built.

Meg is up at first light. It is drizzling, but she will not wear rain gear. It is too hot. She has beans and rice for breakfast because this is all that is available. For her boys she has brought along Cheez Whiz and crackers because they are tired of beans and rice. Unless the Mayan people who live in the nearby village come into the forest with chickens or melons, the menu does not vary. She kisses the boys good-bye and leaves them with her brother, Ed, who helped build the walkway. She puts on a hard hat and climbs into her safety harness. The harness has two six-foot lengths of rope attached. At the end of the ropes are Jumars, or ascenders. Jumars are used in technical rock climbing. The metal U-shaped device has a hinged and grooved gate that allows the rope to slide up as one climbs but locks instantly with downward motion. To descend, the climber must manually push the gate open to allow the rope to slide through.

"Bye, Mom." James waves as he watches his mother begin her climb at the base of the *Ormosia,* or cabbage bark tree.

"Remember, it's our turn next," calls Edward as he watches his mom climb higher.

The boys have accompanied their mother to rainforests all over the world. Now, for the first time, Meg feels they are old enough to go up with her into the canopy. She has ordered special child-size harnesses for them. They are excited, but first their mother has work to do—traps to set for insects, leaves to tag, drawings to make, flowers to count. It will be many hours before they can join her. In the meantime, they can swim in the creek and explore a secret cave that their uncle promises to take them to.

Meg is fast. Within a few short minutes she has ascended 80 feet (24 meters). Then the metal ladders fixed to the *Ormosia* tree run out; for the next 15 feet (4.5 meters) the real climbing begins. Metal staples project from the tree trunk. These are the footholds. For the unpracticed they are scary. They seem spaced too far apart for easy stepping. There is a rhythm. A climber must clip the safety lines securely to wires strung above and then step. Clip, step, unclip one Jumar. Clip, step, unclip again. It is a mosaic of hand- and footwork until Meg is perhaps 95 feet (29 meters) above the ground and approaching the first platform. Meg swings herself onto the platform with the seeming ease of a spider monkey negotiating canopy vines. Now she is at the beginning of the walkway.

The walkway itself is Y-shaped. The main stem of the Y spans nearly one

hundred feet (thirty meters) across Blue Creek to the other bank. Once across, the arms of the Y diverge into two separate walkways that tie into trees on the opposite bank of the creek. There is a major observation platform at the junction of the Y's arms and then others, higher up, that provide views at different levels.

When viewed from below, the canopy appears to be one big maze of tangled vines and foliage, but within the canopy there are a variety of distinct regions. Some might be sunny, some shadier; in some areas the branches of a tree grow at steep angles, while in another region they grow more horizontally. At some points in the canopy there is what researchers call crown shyness, by which they mean the spacing between the crowns of the trees. This spacing influences what lives where in the canopy, providing pathways for toucans and macaws and other creatures that fly. For those creatures that swing or glide or climb, there are the "emerald highways" strung together by vines and lianas that lace the tops of the trees together into a web for commuting life.

Meg has now crossed the creek. She is climbing to the first observation platform, 110 feet (33.5 meters) above the ground. She can hear monkey chatter just above her. She stops, balances on a staple, and looks straight up. There is a sudden dark streak against the sky. Two spider monkeys spring through the branches. They move in fluid loops and arcs, dancing in a tangled rhythm as they alternately grasp with hands, feet, and tail. The space between the branches changes with each new grip, making a shifting geometry against the sky of sliding rectangles, split-second parabolas, and drifting squares. The first monkey pauses at the end of a limb.

Spider monkeys prefer the middle layers of the canopy. The capuchins are often found in the lower levels, and the howler monkeys that bellow at dawn like distant foghorns live at the very top.

Meg begins taking "snapshots" of leaf-eating activity. Last month she had marked every leaf on several branches with a number. She now checks to see how much of each leaf has been eaten.

"Leaf number five is zero percent. Number three is fifty percent. Leaf number four is zero percent, with three minings," Meg calls out to a graduate student assistant, who writes the figures down in a notebook. Mining occurs when an insect eats through just one layer of the leaf's surface, which results in a browning pattern. There might also be galls on a leaf to be noted. In this way Meg acquires her snapshot of leaf-eating activity on particular trees in certain regions of the canopy. She will later compare these figures and notations with what she already knows about the hatching periods of certain insect populations. She has a hunch that the hatchings are synchronized to occur when certain leaves flush, or first grow, and are at their most tender for eating. Through many years of research, Meg has seen a pattern, and her theory is that the newest leaves are the tastiest for insects. Within a matter of two months, 25 percent of the leaf will probably be eaten. The rate slows down as the tender young leaves grow older and tougher.

Meg and her assistant work for the better part of an hour making snapshots of eaten leaves. She then gets out a few mesh bags. It is necessary for a scientist not only to observe ongoing processes but to ask new questions that might only be answered by setting up experiments that often interrupt natural processes. With the mesh bags Meg is going to begin an exclusion experiment. She will tie each bag onto a branch, protecting its leaves from insect predators. Nearby will be another branch without a bag (called a control). She wants to know if by excluding one variable (the leaf-eating insects), the new growth will differ. If there is a barrier, those new leaves will not be eaten, but will this cause even more new leaves to flush out? Or does the fact that a branch's new leaves are being consumed stimulate the tree to produce more?

Meg climbs higher into the canopy. The light twinkles brightly. Above her is a cascade of orchids. Suddenly, through the avenues of emerald light, like winged rainbows two macaws sweep through the canopy. The very air seems splattered with their brilliant color. The birds fly in silence, but the spider monkeys screech in alarm. Branches shake. The bright pair settles in a nearby kapok tree. There might be a nest with chicks in it, for this is the time when the young hatch. Or the pair might be foraging in the surrounding mahogany and kapok trees for fruits and nuts. The beaks of macaws are among the most powerful in the world; macaws can crack almost any nut or seed and also deliver the most wicked of bites. The two birds suddenly explode from the tree like a burst of fireworks and go to another tree nearby. Meg thinks that they are most likely foraging for food to bring to their young. They deliver the food by first chewing it up until it is a pulpy mass that they then swallow and store in a food pouch. When they return to their young, they will regurgitate this food into the mouths of their chicks. Soon they fly off. Meg wishes James and Edward could have seen them.

Meg continues climbing up. She reaches the third platform, 115 feet (35 meters) aboveground. This platform is built in the spreading branches of a *Nargusta* tree. Two lianas snake out along one branch, seeming to choke it in their twisted grip. From this platform she has a good view of four ant gardens she is monitoring as well as of two very special bromeliads.

First she peeks in on the ant gardens. They appear to be almost hanging, with their tendrils of plant roots and vines swaying in the still air. They are actually firmly based on the branches of trees.

"Ah, there's a new one just beginning!" Meg exclaims as she focuses her viewing scope. At the V where one branch joins another, there appears to be a clump of dirt with several small spear-shaped leaves, similar to those of a Christmas cactus, projecting. This, in fact, is the foundation for the little tree-top farms so carefully tended by several different species of ants.

Meg clips her Jumars into some extending cable so she can go higher and get closer to the ant gardens. She wants to observe a mature one that fairly bristles with plant life. Meg counts at least six different kinds of seedling plants here, ranging from orchids to cacti. A *Peperomia* plant forms its base. The ant gardens are magnets for epiphytic growth. Epiphytes, unlike vines or lianas, usually start growing from the canopy down. They need the tree for support. They root on the bark or soil found on the tree. They often begin when a bird excretes a seed from overhead, or as in this case, when the ants themselves drag in bits of plant materials. The bits take root, the seeds sprout. The little ant farmers tend them night and day, and in return they feed off the glucose and proteins that the plants contain in their succaries, the sugary deposits made by the plants' metabolic processes. Scientists think that the ant gardens themselves may be of benefit to more than just the ants, that these gardens help the tree itself by allowing it to capture more solar energy and to trap atmospheric nutrients that might slip off a bare trunk.

There are many such interlocking relationships within the rainforest, and ants often play a major role. Sometimes epiphytic growth can become too much and literally strangle a tree. The bull-horn acacia tree has a very effective defense against epiphytic growth. With its hollow stems it cannot tolerate the stranglehold of many epiphytes. Therefore, it has become the home for a special breed of ants that live in its stems and protect it fiercely. Whenever the tree is even slightly disturbed, the ants charge out of a pinhole on the thorn and attack. In return they feast on the sugar in the tree.

Other ants visit the canopy but live underground in great fungus factories. The leafcutter ants do their farming in reverse, trudging up to the canopy day and night to cut dime-size disks. They then hoist the pieces overhead and carry them back down to underground chambered caverns. In the dark damp maze of tunnels and caves, the leaves begin to grow mold and fungi, which in turn feed the ants. The long, silent lines of tiny, quivering green disks move across the rainforest floor. If you peer closely, you notice that on each disk rides an even smaller ant. This one protects the carrier ant from attacks by deadly micro wasps. For lateral protection alongside the column march lines of larger soldier ants. Each leaf disk, no bigger than a dime and only a fraction of a gram in weight, must get to the fungus factory. Once there, other ants will check the leaves to see if they are right for the kind of fungus the ants are producing. If they are not, the disks are discarded and the ants must turn around and climb one hundred or more feet (thirty meters) into the canopy again in search of the right kind of leaf.

Meg carefully edges her way toward a bromeliad, another kind of epiphyte. An owl butterfly alights on a leaf, then flutters off. A dragonfly hovers like a small jeweled helicopter. At the end of this branch lies a world within a world, a pond within the canopy, a pool hovering midair within a bromeliad.

Bromeliads have spiky leaves, which form a fibrous hollow tank. The outer leaves are bright green, but often the inner leaves are a fiery red and erupt like tongues of flame from a volcano. Rather than lava, however, there is water, and within the water there is life—the larvae of mosquitoes and the tiny tadpoles of a frog, temporarily using the plant's pond as a nursery. The tadpoles, hatched on the ground, slithered onto their mother's back. She then began the long climb in the canopy in search of one of these water nurseries.

Other creatures lurk in the overlapping leaves of the bromeliad. In this bromeliad Meg finds no frogs. Maybe the frog and its tadpoles have been eaten by the little venomous snake she spots coiled among the outer leaves. Perhaps sensing her presence, it slips out of the bromeliad and scrolls across a nearby philodendron leaf—and then holds perfectly still. With its pretty chain-patterned skin, it appears like a beautiful necklace flung out of nowhere. There is a blur of movement in the corner of Meg's eye. A sudden dark design appears from deep within the bromeliad. It is a tarantula. It bristles at this disturbance, climbs toward the bark of the tree, and comes to rest like black embroidery against the bright green leaves.

There is one more bromeliad on this branch. Meg makes her way

toward it and peers in. Out creeps a small tree salamander. Meg is excited. She recognizes it as a very rare lungless salamander. She has only heard about them and seen perhaps one or two pictures. Because of their rareness and their inaccessibility in the canopy, these salamanders with their suction-cup feet are one of the canopy's most mysterious inhabitants. No one knows how they breed, what they eat, or how they live. Meg backs away quickly. She does not want to disturb the creature. She hopes it will return to the maze of bromeliad leaves from which it emerged. This is the surprise she has been looking for to show her boys.

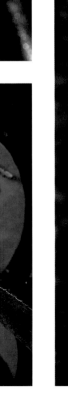

A Column
of Life

MEG AND HER SONS will wait until late afternoon to go up. For this is often when there is a flurry of activity in the canopy as the macaws and toucans fly home to their roosts after foraging and the spider monkeys show off with aerial leaps as the day cools.

So first the boys show Meg the jade green pool in the shadows of a limestone cave carved out by the creek. They swim in and out of its shadows, resting on mossy rocks. Just outside the cave, over the surface of the water, epiphytes drop their aerial roots from one hundred feet (thirty meters) overhead. The banks of the creek here grow thick with moss and strange ferns. And the immense buttressed tree roots are covered with thin veils of bright orange lichen. After swimming, James stands in a slender arrow of sunlight; an owl butterfly lands on his head. He holds very still for almost a minute. He wonders if the butterfly thinks his bright blond hair is a weird flower.

The boys help their mom ferry equipment in the old leaky canoe to the other side of the creek, where she will set up the gear for a column study. Biological diversity means the various and different living things that are found within a community. Although Meg's work is focused on the canopy and the creatures and processes of life that occur within it, she must be able to make a comparison with something else in order to have a true picture of how this part of the machine works. Therefore, on the other side of the river she has marked off several five-meter (16-foot) squares on the forest floor that are situated directly under some of the key observation platforms on the walkway. In Meg's mind this square is like a column that stretches straight up to the canopy. It is her aim to try to inventory, or count, the different species of plants and insects, starting from the ground up.

There have been many methods devised for doing just this. The boys begin by helping another one of Meg's graduate student assistants dig pitfall traps within the square. With spoons and small garden trowels, they dig holes seven or eight inches (18 to 20 centimeters) deep. Into each hole they sink a plastic cup with one inch of alcohol in the bottom of it. By morning they should have a fair sampling of insects that creep across this portion of the forest floor and drop into the cup. With another graduate student Meg counts the trees. She begins at the top of the column with the biggest trees. There are two tall trees, the tops of which reach the canopy. Inside the region known as the understory, which reaches approximately thirty feet (ten meters) in height, there are four different species of trees—a grias, a palm, an acacia, and one she does not know the name of but will look up when she returns to Selby Gardens. These understory trees might someday emerge into the canopy, or they might be crowded out by the young saplings of the next layer down. There are forty-one saplings four or five feet in height struggling toward the filtered light.

Among these forty-one are five different species. Then, just inches above the ground, Meg and her assistant count 197 seedlings. They, too, have begun their struggle toward the light at the top of the canopy.

Continuing to count, Meg finds ten ferns of three different species and forty-one lycopods, or mosses, of which there are five different species. There are also three different kinds of lichen, and on the grias there are thirty-seven epiphytes. By the time Meg and her assistant finish the inventory, they will have counted some 350 plants and two hundred different plant species within this five-meter square. In a temperate forest, such an area might hold a total of fifty plants and at the most thirty different species.

Next Meg needs to sample the kind of insect life that lives just above the ground in the shrubbery. To do this she gets out a beating tray, a shallow screen tray that measures one square meter (nine square feet). While the boys and her graduate assistant hold the tray, she shakes what she estimates to be a cubic meter of foliage for ten seconds. They all count together. At the end of ten seconds, they set down the tray and see what fell from the shrubbery.

"One leafhopper," Meg says, pointing to an insect frantically hopping about on the screen.

"Here's one with really weird jaws," James says as he squints closely at the tray. In this first shake of the foliage, there are also ants, cockroaches, springtails, spiders, and a caterpillar.

They do this two more times with different foliage, all at the same level within the five-meter square.

Next the boys help their mother do a set of sweeps. Sweeping is another technique for sampling insects in the column. The sweeps, however, unlike the pitfall traps or the beating tray, are aimed more at flying insects. Using a butterfly net, Meg aims at a cubic meter of air three or four feet up from the ground. She sweeps the net to the right then to the left. She does this four times, then sets the net down to count her catch. There is one leafhopper, three diptera (flies), and three beetles.

The sweeps, the beating trays, the pitfall traps, and the counting of seedlings, saplings, and trees are all ways for Meg to take "snapshots" of diverse rainforest life.

Finally, when it seems everything in the five-meter square has been accounted for, it is time for the boys to go to the top of the column, to the canopy. They climb expertly into their harnesses. With their mom in the lead and their uncle Ed behind, they begin their ascent. The boys are not in the least nervous, though Meg is. She has left behind all of her note-taking equipment so she can concentrate on the boys' safety. They know not to fool around, argue, or whine. They must think and climb and pay attention.

James and Edward are very excited, for now at last they are going to the place where their mother has gone five days a month, every month of the year, for as long as they can remember. It is a special world. They think of this high, secret place as their mother's world, but they know it is only where she works—it is the canopy, and it belongs to rainforests all over the world on the planet earth. But still they like to think of it as their mom's own special place, and finally, finally they have grown big enough to be let in.

"Oh man, oh man!" exclaims James. He is 87 feet (27 meters) high; his feet are so small he can rest both of them easily on a staple. He has come nose to nose with a bark beetle glittering like an armored knight. It looks like something out of one of his science-fiction comic books. "Weird! Weird! Totally awesome."

"What is it, James?" Meg calls down.

"A beetle. It's beautiful. It's kind of purple—no, sort of gold. Its back is like polished metal, and it's got this weird Darth Vader head on it. Maybe it's poisonous."

"Oh gee, I hope not. Don't touch it. Keep on climbing."

At last they reach the walkway. Meg finds a pen she had left behind and has them help her number a few leaves. Then they climb onto platform three. With their uncle's help they inch out toward the bromeliad.

"Don't touch the tarantula," Meg calls after them.

They see it climb on its jointed legs out of the bromeliad.

"Any frogs in there?" Meg asks.

"Nope," James replies, "but I think I see the salamander."

Edward wishes for the small jeweled venomous snake his mom told him about. There is even a snake that can flatten itself out and sail between the avenues of trees. His mom saw one once when she was working in Cameroon, West Africa.

In Cameroon there were no walkways or staples for footholds. Instead there was an immense inflatable raft that a dirigible floated over the rainforest canopy and settled upon the emergent crown of trees. The raft, like a huge mesh trampoline the size of a baseball diamond, stretched across a wheel-shaped frame of rubber pontoons. Meg reached the raft with a rope; once there, she always wore a safety harness as she hung over the side or walked along the pontoon "streets." The raft made it possible for Meg to sample leaves on the emergent layer of the canopy, a level on which she had never worked before. She also made numerous measurements of a leaf's qualities, such as its toughness and its water content. Meg found that leaf-eating insects consumed significantly less foliage in the upper crowns of trees among the sun leaves when compared to the shade leaves in the middle of the crowns or within the canopy itself.

As fun as this giant trampoline in the sky was, working from it was also grueling. The sun slammed down upon the scientist like a sledgehammer. Temperatures climbed to 120 degrees Fahrenheit (49 degrees Celsius) every day.

The extreme heat was not the worst thing, though, in Meg's mind. Underneath the platform of the tent where she slept at night lurked one of West Africa's deadliest snakes—the Gabon viper. It did not ease her mind to be told that the snake was very shy. Once, in the middle of the night as she made her way to the outhouse, she stepped smack into a battalion of army ants. She screamed bloody murder and woke the entire camp—everyone was sure the Gabon viper had struck. But the army ants with their fierce jaws can deliver a stinging bite that is very painful.

In Panama, at another site, the Smithsonian Tropical Research Institute, there was no raft or walkway. In order to study the "hitchhiker vines" that serve as highways for leaf-eating insects, Meg had to swing through the canopy on a huge construction crane. Standing in a gondola and keeping in radio contact with the crane operator so that he could steer her where she wanted to go, Meg was able to do a thorough study of the vines that linked the canopy trees. In one place, she found a single vine could lace together sixty-four different canopy trees.

That night, after a supper of more beans and rice, peanut-butter-and-jelly sandwiches, and a surprise of Oreo cookies brought all the way from Sarasota, James and Edward take a walk with their mom along a forest trail. The moon, although full, only appears in pieces, a tiny bit at a time, as if diamond chips were scattered through the leaves of the canopy. It is dark and so humid it feels as if you could hold the air in your hands. Thousands of insects flood the air and ground. Safer at night, they come out to feed, flit, and fly. Streams of leaf-cutter ants might still be visible in a chip of moonlight; on the underside of a leaf, another armored beetle, burnished bright as gold, goes silently about its work.

"Look at this!" Edward speaks softly. Gleaming in some low brush is a beautiful spiderweb.

"It moved," whispers James.

"The breeze," says Meg.

"No, Mom, look!" Something very odd is happening to the web. It is not the wind that is moving it. Through some mysterious power, the web is being drawn back into a funnel shape.

"It's the spider, Mom!" James exclaims. Indeed, the spider is winching in its own web by pulling on a line.

Then it is almost as if there is an inaudible *ping*. The web springs back, and at its trembling center is a small insect.

"They must call that a 'slingshot spider'!" Edward exclaims. The boys are thrilled. Meg is astounded. Never before had she seen or even heard of such a spider. They wait for another ten minutes. Two, three, four more times, the spider takes aim with its cunning web and traps another insect.

Meg gets out one of the insect vials filled with alcohol she always carries. With her tweezers she deftly plucks the spider from its web and puts it into the vial.

"Mom!!!" the boys both cry. "You killed it!"

"But we have to take it back. I'm going to send it to the Smithsonian for identification."

"But what if it is the last spider—the very last slingshot spider on earth and now it's dead in a bottle?" James protests.

Meg has an answer for her sons. She points to an identical web and its inhabitant nearby. She has been a scientist working in the field for so long that her first instinct is always to balance the collection of good data with conservation of an unknown species. It is natural curiosity that makes her a scientist, but it is responsible collecting for identification that makes her a *good* scientist. What is permissible, or justifiable, is always a concern—do the ends justify the means? John Audubon, the famous naturalist and bird painter, has always been considered a great artist but today is regarded as an irresponsible environmentalist. He shot thousands of birds, not for identification, not for scientific research, or even for better understanding of a bird's habits, but simply so he could paint the most beautiful picture possible of that bird—a flamingo, an egret, a tern, a pelican, whatever. He might shoot fifty birds of one species in order to create his illusion of nature.

The boys are quiet as they walk back through the forest. Now it is time for bed. While they brush their teeth, Meg traces a leaf and maps the area eaten by insects on graph paper.

When they are all ready, Meg arranges the mosquito netting and then gets out a book for their bedtime stories. It is about pirates. James and Edward love pirates—one-eyed ones, one-legged ones, and of course, those who steal and bury treasure.

"Chapter twenty-nine, 'The Black Spot Again.' " Their mother's voice always sounds the same when she reads the chapter number and title. Then it changes. It becomes her real storytelling voice. She begins: *The council of the buccaneers had lasted some time, when one of them re-entered the house. . . .* " She reads on, " *'There's a breeze coming, Jim,' said Silver. . . .*"

Soon the boys forget the spider in their mother's vial of alcohol. They are thinking about Long John Silver. Is he good, or really, really bad? *Don't trust him, Jim,* they think. *He could kill you.* Both James and Edward think a lot about walking the plank. They often wonder if they could survive, undo the knots. Their mom keeps reading.

The boys' eyelids grow very heavy. The drone of the mosquitoes does not bother them. Edward remembers the velvety tarantula high in the canopy. He wishes they could have seen the venomous snake that looked like a jeweled necklace, but he did see the Darth Vader beetle James found. They all get mixed up with Long John Silver. Their mother's voice grows dimmer.

*"I saw Silver now engaged upon—keeping the mutineers together with one hand, and grasping, with the other, after every means, possible and impossible, to make his peace and save his miserable life. . . ."*

Meg's voice spins out into the night. The words dissolve into the thick, humid air of the rainforest. They become meaningless sounds in the darkness. The palm viper coiled in the buttressed roots of the acacia tree might hear them, but more meaningful is the flick of an anole's tail on a nearby philodendron leaf. An ocelot on the prowl has passed the empty web of the slingshot spider and moves toward the strange sounds. A chameleon clamps two toes on one side of a stem and three on the other and listens to the soft burr of noise from inside, the place it cannot see. In the understory, above the chameleon, a frog slaps its sticky padded feet on a palm frond and freezes— are these the sounds of its enemy, the coati? And far overhead, in the canopy, a fruit bat cocks its sonar toward the dark little cabin one hundred feet below as it swoops through the night dropping a seed here, a seed there. The words, the strange sounds, melt into the night as a tiny bromeliad begins to grow in silence and invisibility high above. The bat flies on.

The boys are sound asleep. Meg walks out onto her porch and down the steps to the ground. The rain has begun again, as it so often begins, with single, separate drops, sounding more like thuds than the tinny *plink*s of city rain. It is a round sound, so round and so liquid that it is easy to imagine the shape of each raindrop as it splashes and flattens on a broad leaf in the top of the canopy. Within these first few seconds, she can actually hear the rain high up before she can feel it. But the drops continue, finding their way down through the layers. The clouds let loose bellyfuls of moisture. One rain sphere slides into another, until the water falls in thin strands. Within minutes it is beating down so hard that the thin silvery strands lose their shape, turning to liquid smoke that clouds the air.

Meg goes back onto her porch and lights her Coleman lamp. She gets out her computer, and in the dim, foggy night of the rainforest a small neon-green rectangle is illuminated. She needs to enter the latest figures on the leaf-

eating patterns that she has mapped on the graph paper as well as yesterday's insect inventories.

She is alone. Meg spends much of her time alone in the canopy and then back on the forest floor, pondering what she has seen above. But despite the solitariness of her work, the lonely hum of the computer, and the clicking of the keys, in the back of her mind is the consoling knowledge of other scientists and pioneers. It is easy for her to bridge the chasm of more than one hundred years and reach out toward the one who navigated the path to freedom by feeling for the moss on the north sides of trees. Were Harriet Tubman's experiences so different from her own? Didn't they both have to trust their knowledge of the earth and find their way through a tangled darkness?

It has been a long day, an anxious one with the kids up in the canopy, but the very thought of Harriet Tubman is strangely reassuring. So Meg types on through the next several hours until her computer batteries begin to fade and the gray of a new dawn filters slowly through the canopy. In just another few hours it will be time for her to climb into her safety harness and navigate her way up once more through the understory and into the canopy, for another day of work on this, the last frontier of the rainforest.

# Glossary

**biological diversity** or **biodiversity** The measurement of the number of different living things that are found in one particular area.

**bromeliad** Mainly epiphytic plants that often form rosettes of leaves.

**canopy** The upper layer of foliage of a forest, usually about 60 to 100 feet (18 to 30 meters) above the forest floor.

**crown** The very topmost foliage and branches of a tree.

**crown shyness** The spacing between the crowns of the trees. This spacing provides pathways for a variety of creatures that leap or fly through the treetops.

**emergent tree** A very tall tree with a crown that extends above the canopy growth.

**epiphytes** Any of the various plants that grow on other plants for support and draw their nourishment from the air and rain.

**flush** The earliest or first growth of leaves on a tree or plant.

**galls** Small bumps or abnormal growths on plants caused by insects, fungi, or bacteria.

**herbarium** A library for plants in which the various parts of a plant, such as its leaves or petals, are pressed and may be preserved so researchers can study them.

**herbivory** Leaf and plant eating by insects and other animals.

**leafcutter ants** A tropical species of ants that live and work communally in the epiphytic gardens known as ant gardens.

**lianas** High-climbing vines that are abundant in the rainforest. They begin as seedlings on the forest floor and eventually climb to the canopy, where they interlace into networks of woody loops and links to form a kind of highway.

**mining** A browning pattern on a leaf where an insect has eaten through just one layer of the leaf's surface.

**pavilion** The very highest layer of growth in the rainforest formed by the crowns of the trees that emerge above the canopy.

**photosynthesis** The process by which the chlorophyll cells of a plant convert light into chemical energy.

**temperate forest** A forest in the earth's temperate zones, where the climate is neither extremely hot nor extremely cold.

**understory** The lower, relatively open region of a rainforest that reaches from ground level up to about thirty feet (ten meters) in height. The plants that survive in this region are shade tolerant.